Dear Parent:
Your child's love of reading starts here!

Every child learns to read in a different way and at his or her own speed. Some go back and forth between reading levels and read favorite books again and again. Others read through each level in order. You can help your young reader improve and become more confident by encouraging his or her own interests and abilities. From books your child reads with you to the first books he or she reads alone, there are I Can Read Books for every stage of reading:

SHARED READING
Basic language, word repetition, and whimsical illustrations, ideal for sharing with your emergent reader

BEGINNING READING
Short sentences, familiar words, and simple concepts for children eager to read on their own

READING WITH HELP
Engaging stories, longer sentences, and language play for developing readers

READING ALONE
Complex plots, challenging vocabulary, and high-interest topics for the independent reader

ADVANCED READING
Short paragraphs, chapters, and exciting themes for the perfect bridge to chapter books

I Can Read Books have introduced children to the joy of reading since 1957. Featuring award-winning authors and illustrators and a fabulous cast of beloved characters, I Can Read Books set the standard for beginning readers.

A lifetime of discovery begins with the magical words "I Can Read!"

Visit www.icanread.com for information
on enriching your child's reading experience.

For the Rossi family,
looking forward to our
next vacation.
—A.L.

I Can Read Book® is a trademark of HarperCollins Publishers.

Chicken on Vacation
Copyright © 2018 by HarperCollins Publishers
All rights reserved. Printed in the United States of America.
No part of this book may be used or reproduced in any manner whatsoever without written permission except
in the case of brief quotations embodied in critical articles and reviews. For information address HarperCollins
Children's Books, a division of HarperCollins Publishers, 195 Broadway, New York, NY 10007.
www.icanread.com

Library of Congress Control Number: 2017954082
ISBN 978-0-06-236419-7 (trade bdg.)—ISBN 978-0-06-236418-0 (pbk.)

22 23 24 CWM 10 9 8 7
❖
First Edition

CHICKEN on VACATION

By Adam Lehrhaupt
Pictures by Shahar Kober

HARPER
An Imprint of HarperCollinsPublishers

Zoey burst into the barn.

"Pack your hat, Sam!" she said.

"We're going on a beach vacation!"

"We'll swim!"

"We'll build sand castles!"

"We'll find buried treasure!"

"What about lunch?" asked Sam.

"You didn't mention lunch."

"I packed a picnic," said Zoey.

"Why didn't you say so?" asked Sam.

"Let's go!"

"Where are you going?" asked Pip.

"On vacation!" said Zoey.

"Come to the beach with us!"

"Will there be crabs?" asked Pip.

"Crabs can pinch."

"I'll protect you," said Zoey.

"No pinching on my watch!"

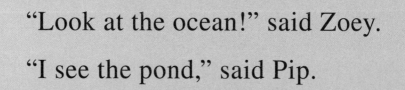

"Look at the ocean!" said Zoey.

"I see the pond," said Pip.

"Look at the beach!" said Zoey.

"I see dirt," said Pip.

Pip swam in the pond.

Sam swam in the mud.

Zoey swam Zoey-style.

"You're on the dock," said Pip.

"Not the dock," said Zoey.

"A surfboard!"

Sam shook.

"Is it time for lunch?" he asked.

"Time for sand castles!" said Zoey.

"I brought tools."

Pip built a short castle.

Sam built a wide castle.

Zoey built a Zoey castle.

"My kingdom is grand!" said Zoey.

"My kingdom is messy," said Pip.

"My kingdom is for lunch!" said Sam.

"I found something," said Pip.

"A map!" said Zoey.

"It leads to buried treasure."

"And lunch?" asked Sam.

But Zoey was already off.

"Where's the treasure?" asked Sam.

"I see the tractor," said Pip.

"Not the tractor," said Zoey.

"A lookout tower!"

Zoey climbed to the top.

"I see the treasure!" she said.

"It's that way."

"I see an old fence," said Pip.

"Not a fence," said Zoey.

"A shipwreck!"

"A shipwreck?" asked Sam.

"The treasure must be nearby."

"I see a rock," said Pip.

"Not a rock," said Zoey.

"A giant crab!"

"It IS a giant crab!" said Pip.

"It'll pinch me!"

"I'll protect you!" said Zoey.

"Take THAT, crab!"

"You scared it!" said Sam.

"You saved me," said Pip.

"Told you I would," said Zoey.

"And THERE'S the treasure!"

"Pie!" squealed Sam.

"The treasure is pie!"

"Ready for our picnic?" asked Zoey.

"I'm always ready," said Sam.

31

While Sam and Pip enjoyed pie,
Zoey made plans for tomorrow.